visited
by a tiger

# part I

This is the so-called handy hand model of the brain developed by Dr. Dan Siegel, which offers us a simplified representation of the functioning and structure of the brain.

And so,
if you imagine that
my arm symbolizes the
*spinal cord*→1
that runs up to the base
of the skull
and
the palm of my hand
represents the *brain stem*,→2
that's responsible for survival, for keeping us alive,

keeping our heart beating and keeping us breathing and

water levels and temperature levels of the body.
And then

the thumb symbolizes what's called the *limbic system.*[→3]

And this is the emotional, motivational, memory part of the brain.

The fingers symbolize the newest part of the brain: the *thinking brain.*[→4]

Now, our maximal functioning occurs when *all of these parts of the brain are working together.*[→6]

So what happens as we go about our day to day activities:

one or the other part takes over or dominates the functioning.

This part, *mid part of the brain,*→2+3

which is designed to keep us safe, to keep us functioning, is like the watchdog of the brain.

So, as we're going about our day to day activities, it is on alert for any potential threat or danger.

And it's on alert for, you know, what is working well and is well.

But when there is some
kind of threat
—that threatens our lives,
our well-being in general,
this *mid part of the brain*[→2+3]
is designed to automatically
cope with that threat, what's
called the Fight-Flight-
Freeze and Faint response.

And when that happens,
this mid part of the brain,
the *limbic system*[→2] and the
*brain stem,*[→3]
they alert the brain to take
certain actions
in terms of blood flow and
oxygen flow to certain parts
of the body.

So, this is a time when the heart rate is increased, the blood pressure increases, the flow of blood to the extremities is increased.

This is a time when there is less blood flow to the non-essential systems

like digestion and reproduction for example.

And when this happens that this *mid part of the brain*[→2+3] is alerted and preparing us to take action,

the *thinking brain*[→4] goes offline—often referred to as *“we flip our lid”*[→5]—

because this is the slower part, the newer part,

that is too slow to deal with any emergency that is happening.

So it's not a time to be thinking and analyzing and trying to understand and plan.

It is more of a time for action.

And under proper circumstances, when the threat is taken care of, the tiger has been defeated or the boss is calmed down,

then the body naturally goes back to a more *integrated and stable state.*→6

But often-times especially when the emotions are extremely high or at times

when there is a constant bombardment of stress, (whether that's actual stress or just imagined stress),

then we have a *state of constant arousal.*[→5]

And this is the time when impairment of various parts of the body can occur.

Because we are not built to be under that *constant state of arousal.*[→5]

And so this is, where

stress actually can kill.

# part II

You were going about preparing all the equipment and I was sitting quietly and milling around. At rest, integrated, we were both *feeling comfortable, warm* and *balanced.*[→6]

Then with the book that you gave me,
we started this conversation about racism.
And I knew already that this was an area
that I kind of keep it at a distance
because I can become very quickly, *emotionally aroused.*[→5]

But we entered that
conversation
and got deeper into that
conversation
and all of the pain and
suffering, struggle that is
associated with that for me
started quickly to emerge.

Before I even knew it,
this *calm homeostatic
state*[→6] had changed,
where this *emotional
part,*[→3]
the survival part of my
brain was signaling “threat”.
So, as this emotional side
is signaling: “We’re entering
some territory here”

and then that sort of *thinking brain*→[4]—that might've kept me more on target about

what, you know, we were about to do—

suddenly it was *offline.*→[5]

And so what I found was, that suddenly I'm talking about my father,

about the racism he experienced,

about his deep anger and aggression that was often the topic of the conversations in our home.

So, that fight in me was coming more and more to the surface.

It was as if suddenly
I had been *visited by
a tiger*[→5]
standing in front of me
and, and my body was say-
ing, you know, my heart is …
is racing more and I just
feel the heat in my body just
in preparation to fight.
So, as happens when
that fight is preparing me
to deal with whatever I’m
dealing with,
again, the best thinking is
not happening.

The brain in general
reacts the same way
whether the threat is an
actual one,

whether it’s an imagined one.

And this is what is

so often the case today

because we don’t have those animal predators that are the threats to us.

It is more *the psycho-logical, the emotional, the social threats*[→5]

that we can experience so quickly as we did in that conversation.

So quickly and so frequently as we go about our day to day business.

All of this *emotional activity*[→3] is important.

And I think especially as people of color,
just in this environment as more people of color are here in Berlin.
As, you know, they’re welcomed by a certain population,
but then hated by another substantial part of the population.

The purpose of the *emotional brain*[→3] working together with the *brain stem*[→2] is
that it keeps us alive and it keeps us functioning and keeps us safe.

So if, that *emotional brain*[→3] was not alerting us to,
you know, what's going on and what's safe, what's not safe, what's threatening, what's good, what's bad,
then, you know, we would be at loss, at a loss to take care of ourselves in the ways that we need to.

For me, just, in terms of my personal survival
and my work as a psychologist,
the survival of my people in general
that focus on survival is what is foremost in my mind and in my work.[→6]

This artists' book by Anike Joyce Sadiq is based on the eponymous video piece and a conversation with Dr. phil. Lula Morton Drewes who dedicated her professional work to assist people in learning to bring the *thinking brain* back online in times of emotional arousal. Sound by music producer and artist Lamin Fofana.

The special edition includes a vinyl record.

first edition
2020
edition taube

isbn
978-3-945900-49-9